10 THINGS WHITE PEOPLE DON'T TELL YOU

Otis Aubert

Otisaubert.com

Copyright © 2017 Otis Aubert, Memphis

ISBN: 9781520540948

Table of Contents

CHAPTER I

I am white.

I cannot— and will not— speak on anything "black."

I will not pretend to know what blacks do, think, and feel.

I can— and will— speak on what white people do, think, and feel.

How do I know?

Here are my credentials:

I am white.
My parents are white.
My wife is white.
My kids are white.
My siblings are white.
My friends are white.

I have done business with, worked with, and been around white people for over forty years, all kinds of whites: liberal, conservative, fat, skinny, smart, and stupid.

I am simply here to share what white people think, but do not say to people of color.

This book will include a lot about race, racism, and racists. So, before we go any further, I need to define a word:

rac·ism
ˈrāˌsizəm/

noun
   prejudice, discrimination, or antagonism directed against someone of a different race based on the belief that one's own race is superior.

That word will be used many times throughout this book, and I wanted to define it early so we are on the same page. Words have meanings, and if those meanings can be changed by a certain group, the meaning of that word becomes the property of that group.

When a group owns a word, they can modify the definition to suit an agenda. That word then becomes a weapon, and the truth of the word becomes lost. The meanings must be the same for all people if those people are ever to unite. It is impossible for two sides to come to agreement or understanding if they define the same word two different ways. Especially a powerful word like racism.

Two stories about words:

Story number one:

When I was in junior high, there was an ongoing debate between the black kids and the black teachers. The school I attended was about half black and half white (teachers and students). It was right around the time Gangsta rap was gaining popularity, and the N-Word was flying around like a swarm of angry bees. But the end of the word was modified, having an "a" in place of the e and r.

The argument presented by the teachers was that the kids were embarrassing themselves and their people by throwing around the N-word like it meant nothing, showing their ignorance in not knowing the importance of the word, and in turn, disrespecting the pain their people had suffered and the sacrifices their people had made for the kids themselves.

The kids had a different point of view. They argued that the N-Word had too much strength, and they were rendering it powerless through saturation. How much punch could a word that people use as a common pronoun have? The kids believed they were taking ownership of the word and modifying its definition.

Who was right?

We may never know.

The folks who agreed with the teachers seem to have won the debate, and returned the N-Word to what they believed was its rightful place as the most taboo word in history.

Story number two:

Two of my friends and I were sitting at a bar one evening. We were discussing sports, wives, kids, and so on. One of my white friends (let's call him Jack) mentioned that black and white people have a different smell. My other friend, being white also (let's call him Mike), took offense to this notion, saying, "That was racist." "It's not racist; it's the truth," Jack replied and continued, "Are you saying you have never smelled the difference between white people and black people?" "No, I haven't," Mike replied, becoming more agitated.

They went back and forth for a while. Jack would say things like, "Have you ever gotten close enough to smell one?" Have you never been to a black person's house?" And Mike would say things like, "If there is a difference, I have never noticed." And, "You just don't really like black people, and you find whatever you can to separate them from us." Finally, they turned to me and asked what I thought.

"Well," I said, "The blacks that I played ball with said we all smell like bologna and wet dog."

They both just stared at me, each thinking something very different, I assume.

1. Whites believe the word "racism," will soon be rendered powerless, and it will be black people's fault.

I am going to attempt to define a new word, or maybe it's been coined before. I don't really know.

White Station

noun
1.
the social or official position of the Caucasian race within any certain society in relation to other ethnic groups.

2.
the way of life and quality of life Caucasians have within any certain society.

2. Whiteguy will never truly threaten his station.

Now, this does not mean white people will only help whites, only vote for whites, and only hire whites. On the contrary; they will do whatever they can to improve their *personal* station first, and rarely will that threaten the overall White Station.

Example:

Whiteguy has no problem hiring a person of color if he thinks it would improve his business, thereby improving his personal station. In many ways, this also protects the White Station by appeasing a group that could revolt and threaten the White Station.

But Whiteguy would never hire more people of color than whites, or hire a person of color to a management position if he suspected they would only promote and hire other people of color. This is because Whiteguy believes that person is a threat to his personal station and the White Station. His personal station being his way of life (his current station in the business) and the White Station (the foundation of his way of life, and the foundation of the way of life for his descendants).

Whites believe their station was fought for, died for, killed for, sacrificed for, planned for, worked for, and everything you can image for; and they would never dishonor their ancestors by giving away the keys to the castle.

White people believe they are the descendants of those who created western civilization, and they are responsible for protecting it.

If you directly ask an educated white person about the prior paragraphs, you will probably hear something like, "It's not about race. It's about ideology. I align with people who share my ideology, not my race. It just so happens, some ideological lines run parallel with racial divides."

This is BS.

Why does he lie?

Because Whiteguy believes he is stuck between a rock and a hard place. But he believes he is stuck because blacks stuck themselves first.

I'll explain.

Whiteguy sees blacks openly discuss sticking together. He sees them vote together. He sees their ideology being united. He hears them openly advocate for minority owned businesses, and he hears them advocate to have more people of color in positions of power. So, what makes him think that trend would not continue in perpetuity?—blacks favoring blacks in promotion, contracts, etc.

Whiteguy understands this strategy and feels no anger towards blacks for this. But why would Whiteguy knowingly help any group that would leave his group out?

So, why does Whiteguy feel blacks stuck themselves first?
Because they fought for acceptance.

Whiteguy does not understand this. For Whiteguy, the only reasonable options are to either assimilate or separate. Whiteguy would never fight for acceptance. He does not understand why anyone would fight for acceptance from a group who enslaved them. Whiteguy believes he would only fight for sovereignty.

Whiteguy believes the blacks skipped a few steps, and in return, stuck themselves between needing white acceptance (the rock) and not having their own sovereign state (the hard place), because they chose not to assimilate *or* separate.

Let me remind you, I am not saying what is right or wrong, simply what Whiteguy thinks.

You might be saying, "Of course, they fought for their freedom!"

Well, I guess we would need to define *fought*, and at that, *freedom*:

Fight I

American Revolutionary War:

Total casualties: Over 30,000
Result: Freedom from British rule, the Bill of Rights, Americans in complete control over their economy/society, etc.

Fight II

World War II:
Total causalities: Over 60,000,000

Results: Freedom from the Axis power's expansionist interests for the entire globe. Returned sovereignty and created sovereignty for many nations.

Fight III

American Civil Rights ~~War~~ Movement:

Total casualties: A nonviolent movement (minimal). Result: Laws passed to ensure equal rights for minorities. No sovereignty for an African-American nation. No reparations.

So, who says violence never solves anything?

Everybody.

But it's simply not true.

3. Whiteguy defines freedom as sovereignty not acceptance.

Not the right to vote,
Or the right to free speech.
Or the right to sit at the front of the bus.

But to be a complete, self-governing state.

In 1865, President Lincoln approved an order to redistribute 400,000 acres of land along the South Carolina, Georgia, and Florida coast to the newly freed slaves, to be owned by blacks and controlled by blacks. By June, 40,000 blacks had settled on the 400,000 acres.

But shortly after, Lincoln's successor, Andrew Johnson, repealed the order and returned the land to the previous land owners.

Just imagine if the newly freed slaves had the time and resources to acquire weapons. A 40,000 man/woman/child armed front is a significant force.

Not to mention sympathizers and other unknown allies that could have been negotiated.

Who could imagine what America would look like today if they had kept that land?

We will never know.

Now, imagine if sentiments had swayed towards Malcom X instead of Martin Luther King, Jr. during the Civil Rights Movement.

The result? Again, no one will ever know.

But we do know one thing;
the result of the peaceful approach.

Whiteguy believes Malcom X's philosophy would have been more effective than King's.

Whiteguy believes the Black American herd mentality has been a large part of their degradation.

It might seem empowering at first, but in the end, a herd is still just a herd, waiting to be picked off one by one.

4. Whiteguy believes Control begins with power.

And power begins with weapons;
And weapons insure control over land;
And land is everything.

When you begin to read Genesis, you quickly understand that all of the "He begat her" and "He begat him" is simply a claim on land. Just like today, land passes down the family chain.

Christians and Muslims have been in a land war for over 1400 years. Every war I can think of has been fought over land. Land is the foundation for a society.

5. Whiteguy believes assimilation would have been the most effective and efficient choice to improve the black quality of life.

Whites believe assimilation would have forced acceptance though examples of equality. Asians are a perfect example. They have not pushed for an Asian culture to be accepted inside America. They do not unite in their vote or their ideology. For the most part, they have assimilated.

The result?

The median Asian American income is more than the average Caucasian American. In fact, all other races have a higher median income than blacks. Whites believe this happened because those other races concentrated on work, assimilation, education and family. Not on acceptance.

You might say that proves an opposite point. You might say that shows proof of the systematic oppression of blacks. You might say you cannot compare an Asian that has immigrated to America to a black person that was born here and suffered the visible and invisible oppression that the White Station has inflicted.

You're right. I can't compare the two; and I'm not. I am illustrating why Whiteguy believes in assimilation over acceptance. He has seen assimilation work and multiculturalism fail.

CHAPTER II

6. Whites believe the black vernacular is the second biggest reason black people are being left behind.

"I can't have someone representing my company that can't even speak the language correctly."

This is by far the most popular reason I hear from my white business owner friends as to why they do not, or cannot, hire blacks.

Whiteguy believes some blacks think they are taking a stand or uniting in some sort of rebellion against speaking "white" by speaking a slang version of English. He believes most blacks view it as an art form that shows an independent, unified culture. But he thinks they are dead wrong.

He believes, "We all speak English…blacks just speak it incorrectly." Whiteguy argues that it doesn't represent a counter-culture rising from the depths to gain a righteous, separate respect. It represents ignorance.

The international language of business is English, and it's the most spoken language in the developed world.

If blacks really want to make a white racist's heart jump, they should speak the language correctly.

The white racist smiles inside when blacks speak Ebonics. It's like an insurance policy, ensuring that blacks remain the underclass.

Imagine if Whiteguy's New York art gallery had a position open in reception. They received three applications. The first applicant was a well-spoken, black female from Harlem with a high school diploma. The second applicant was a white, female art history major from Arkansas with the thickest southern accent you have ever heard. The third was a black, female, college-educated woman in her thirties with a medium Ebonics accent.

Who got the job?

The well-spoken black woman from Harlem, of course.

Whiteguy believes anyone can be trained. His skills are in the art world, not speech pathology.

Now, should the more qualified white lady from Arkansas sue the art gallery or concentrate on passing laws about accent discrimination?

14

Whiteguy believes she should learn to lose the accent if she wants to work in a New York gallery. That effort would produce faster and better results for her and the gallery.

You might say she could sue them and get a lot of money. She could put that gallery out of business, open her own gallery with the money, and in the process, set a precedent for accent discrimination.

But she wanted to work for a New York art gallery, not put one out of business and open one that would probably fail because the clientele would be apprehensive at best in buying from a southerner. So, in that scenario, she is not getting what she wants. She sacrifices for an ideology, not for a strategy—always a mistake in Whiteguy's mind.

You might say, "That's not right! It's unfair and just plain wrong." And you might be right. But the question I'm addressing is not if it's right or wrong, but what's the best way to fix it.

Let's stray from assimilation for a bit and play:

Who's the racist?

I attended a public school in the south. I'm not sure how long it had been going on prior to my attendance, but the school participated in busing. Half of our students were white kids from the suburbs, and the other half were black kids from the inner city.

I had my first experience with a liberal in my seventh grade civics class. I did not know he was a liberal because I had never met one, or ever heard that word.

He was the teacher—an educated, white man who had spent most of his life in academia. I did not know there was anything askew until one day, when he was lecturing the class, he seemed upset. He said, "Look around you. Do you notice anything strange about the class?" "No—no," the class responded. "Take a better look. Look at who you are sitting next to." His voice grew louder and more frustrated. "Half of the class is white, and half is black. Now, why are all the blacks sitting on one side and the whites on the other? This is the problem in America."

As he went on, he grew more agitated. He preached about busing, how it had been long enough, and how not enough progress being made. He even slanted to the position that whites were separating themselves because they are inherently racist. He picked out one of the white girls in the class and asked why she had never sat next to or tried to make friends with one of the blacks. As you can imagine, she was very embarrassed and mumbled a convoluted response.

Finally, in the middle of his rant, one of the black kids raised his hand, and the teacher called on him ever so sweetly. The student seemed a little angry and said, "What makes you think we want to sit with the white kids?"

The class giggled and laughed.
  So, who's the racist?
  The white girl?
  The black guy?
  The giggling class?

  Whiteguy thinks it's the teacher.

  Had it never occurred to this teacher that the blacks
never wanted to come out to the suburbs in the first
place? To be around a bunch of kids that they had
nothing in common with? Had he never considered that
the blacks *chose* to congregate among each other? Had he
never thought that forcing two races to be together might
be counterproductive? No, he hadn't. Whiteguy believes
the teacher only wants to give to a perceived underclass
to feel better about himself.

  The teacher believes that they need his help.
  Therefore, he is racist.

  To let blacks and whites intermingle naturally would
leave him out of the equation. He could not be superior to
anyone. He would much rather give fish to the needy than
teach the needy to fish. Partly, because he doesn't actually
care about the needy (only how said giving makes him
feel about himself), and partly because the credit he
would receive from the teaching would not be
acknowledged immediately, if ever.

THE SEVEN SHADES OF WHITE:

I. Liberal Racist:

> This is the racist from the previous story. The ego-driven intellectual whose world revolves around validating their own intelligence and morality. They blame everything on the conservatives.

II. Liberal Non-racist:

> We all know this guy. He just wants to get high and have good feelings among all children of ~~god~~ mother earth. They can't decide who to blame, but they're pretty sure it's the rural whites.

III. Conservative Racist:

> Also known as the redneck, white-trash, or the small-town racist. They know not what they do. They are sheltered and suffer from ignorance. They blame everything on the liberals.

IV. Conservative Non-racist:

> They represent the majority of whites in this country. They are concerned with making their mortgage payments and instilling a moral foundation in their children. They do not believe that they were the cause of the current racial divide, nor is it their responsibility to fix. They believe that they barely have the time and capital to handle their own

problems, much less anyone else's. They believe that a person's life is the culmination of that person's choices, regardless of what they were born into. They blame the individual.

V. Hipster:

Shallow and totally self-involved, they have no spine, so they have no opinions of their own. They must steal their identity from others. Totally submerged in fad and political correctness, they blame whoever was the butt of the latest satirical narrative.

VI. Workaholic:

These people rarely think about color. They see one thing (their work), and that one thing is their god. They don't blame. They don't have time to.

VII. The Angry Racist:

The angry racist hates. They deny that something inside is broken. They feel sadness—a sadness akin to despair— a sorrow so self-destructive that it must to be released, so it manifests as anger, which evolves into hate.

Given the prior list, it would seem that 43% of whites are racist. This might be true depending on where you look. But I find that it's usually about 20%. I say that because whenever I'm in a group of ten Whities, two are usually racist. But the real number may even be lower.

Why? Because the true racist believes a certain race is inferior or superior to another race. *That is it.* There are no variations. That is the only meaning.

Believe it or not, the vast majority of members of the prior list are not racist, even though *racist* was in the title. It was in the profile because that is how their group behaves and is, therefore, perceived.

How do I know this?

Because I see how they are intimidated by a confident black person. I see how they embrace black culture, and, in a lot of ways, prefer it.

How can you believe a race is inferior when you are intimidated by them and admire what they have created and accomplished. I argue that you can't. You can act like it, but you can't believe it.

To believe it, you must be isolated in your own culture (which is very rare now, given the internet). Or just plain angry (hateful).

Apathy is not racism.

Most educated Whiteguys—liberal or conservative—know that the best way out of poverty is education. But not the education you learn in school; the type you learn from successful people. The type that teaches you how employers create slaves and how to obtain *real* freedom. The type that teaches you about the division of labor and specialization. The type that teaches **how** money makes money, how business works, how it's a game, and how identifying the object of the game is part of the game. The type that teaches you if you can't speak the language correctly, you are at a massive disadvantage. The type that teaches you how taxes, lending, collateral, the economy, etc.; how it all works.

So, why do white liberals and conservatives not make strong efforts to teach this to minorities?

Because neither *really* care.

The conservatives don't teach these things because, like I said before, they don't think it's their problem, and because they believe people of color are very, and, in a lot of cases, more capable of pulling themselves up by their own boot straps. And like I said before, some also believe that people of color would stick together, becoming an opposition to the White Station.

The Liberals don't teach this because the benefits they receive do not outweigh the comforts they give up. They believe talking and bringing issues to public forums, protesting, and posting on social media meet their self-designated responsibility. How many times have you heard a liberal say, "At least we have opened the lines of dialog," or "The first step is to talk about it."? Yet, they show little to no action. That reveals their motivation. They get to hear themselves talk, profess their morality, receive the admiration of others, and have their righteousness and intellect validated. But they sacrifice nothing. It's a win-win.

CHAPTER III

7. Whites will take any color slave

Am I going to try and convince you slavery is not racist?

You better believe it.

Please refresh your memory on the actual definition of racism before we continue.

rac·ism
ˈrāˌsizəm/

noun
prejudice, discrimination, or antagonism directed against someone of a different race based on the belief that one's own race is superior

Society is built on labor. It must have it in order to survive. Slavery, in one form or another, has been a means of attaining labor since the beginning of civilization. Throughout history, slaves have been many colors and races. Free labor was the most valuable thing in the world. Why would anyone narrow the priceless free labor market with skin color regulations?

They wouldn't.

Racism was simply one excuse to attain free labor.

Modern slavery is a bit more complicated, being that human rights are widely recognized and all. Slave labor had to change in order to survive. It had to take control over its definition. It had to modify its name;

"Cheap Labor"
Much more morally acceptable, right?
But make no mistake, cheap labor is slave labor.

Cheap labor made a run in America for a good while, and still does with some illegal immigrants and in certain areas of the economy. But for the most part, it had to move on. It was no longer welcome.

So, cheap labor had to find a place to go. It had to find a place where it would be nurtured, far from the reach of unions and from a people who could assemble and possess guns.

The third world.

But as economies grow, they need more than just cheap physical labor to build on. They need labor in all forms to construct a framework strong enough to support itself as it expands.

And with any type of labor, a slave is always preferred... regardless of color.

But due to the bill of rights, civil rights, and all sorts of legal protections, these new slaves had to be slaves by choice, or at least think it was a choice.

So, the economy went to work. It innovated and grew. It hired workers and created markets never imagined. It taxed income, land, and business, pulling everyone into its web, from the homesteader to the warrior. It propagandized; "More is Better." It created and borrowed money to grow faster. It complicated and condensed power. It drove down its workers' real wages and increased their liabilities.

It successfully created paid slaves—a labor force able to fuel it into eternity.

A Portrait of One of the Many Types of Modern Paid Slaves:

If an employer ever offers to pay you more than the going wage for your skill, or lack thereof, you might be slave material.

Why would you be slave-ready if you are offered more money? Doesn't that mean you are special? Better than the competition, extremely likable? He's paying you more because you're so awesome, and he doesn't want another company picking you up, right?

You might think so. It does make sense. But hear me out.

Most employers are looking for slaves, not employees. Especially not employees who don't need them.

I'll explain.

Employer A (let's call them Acme Bricklayers) is interviewing candidate A (let's call him Bill the Bricklayer). Acme has already gone through Bill's social media posts, background checks, credits reports, etc. Acme sees that Bill is a good Bricklayer. His past employers have good things to say about him. Acme knows Bill runs thin margins with his finances from his credit reports. They see that Bill drives a car, owns a house, and has clothes that project a certain status. Acme sees he is proud of this status through posts of vacations, sporting and social events.

Acme feels like the perception of status, money, and freedom are more valuable to Bill than actual money, status, and freedom, so Acme really only has a few questions for Bill. These questions are to validate what Acme feels could be a possibility. The possibility of Bill becoming a slave, and maybe even the perfect slave.

.

Acme asks Bill questions like, "What do you like to do in your spare time? What would your goals be at Acme if you got the job? What are your life goals?"

These questions are not to determine if Bill would be a team player or to get to know Bill better as a person. These questions are to decipher what Bill's motivations are—what he holds true value in.

If Acme feels Bill's answers reflect his motivations are for his family relationships, freedom, self-sufficiency, virtues, etc., slavery might not be an option for Bill.

But let's say Bill's answers reflect additional shallowness.

Then Acme might offer Bill more than the going rate for Bricklayers. "Wow! You seem like a perfect fit for this company. We don't want to lose you, so we are able to offer you 15% more than the standard rate."

Bill is flattered and excited. That's an extra $750.00 per month.

Bill takes the job then and there.

Acme is excited too. They might have a possible slave coming aboard, because Acme believes Bill will further extend his spending and debt to meet or exceed the extra $750.00 per month.

Thus, putting himself in a position where he *needs* the extra 15 % wage.

In the beginning, Acme portrays the work environment as a family environment. The management often drops words like: family, loyalty, and team. This makes Bill feel secure, like he is part of something bigger and greater than himself.

But as time goes on, Acme demands more and more from Bill. More clock time and more labor, and at first, Bill does not mind. He is being paid more than average, so he feels he should return the favor.

But Acme continues to push Bill in an attempt to find the apex of his productivity. Soon, Bill becomes frazzled and stressed. He asks for help or maybe fewer hours per week. His requests are met with graciousness and consideration, but there always seems to be something out of management's control as to why the time is not right.

Bill grows angry. He begins to look for alternative work. He scans the wanted ads and calls other bricklaying companies to see if they are hiring.

Bill is soon able to get interviews at a few of those companies. But he quickly realizes those companies are not willing to pay the extra $750.00 that Bill now **needs.**

A week or so later, Acme Manager #3 calls Bill into his office. He tells Bill they are going to lower his hours and give him an extra week of vacation.

Bill is relieved and thankful. He feels renewed and respected (a little). He begins to work with more enthusiasm and efficiency, like he did when he started.

He makes no adjustment in his finances, because he feels better. He does not cut expenses or take on extra work in order to reduce debt and attain financial security.

Just like Acme is betting on.

Everyone is happy.

What Bill doesn't realize is Acme Manager #3 received a call from his friend who works at one of the companies that Bill interviewed with. That friend told Manager#3 that Bill was looking for alternative work.

Manger #3 knew then that Bill had surpassed his productivity apex, so he made a small adjustment to Bill's schedule to bring him closer to this goal.

Bill still does the work of an employee, plus a third, but now he is happy about it.

At least for a while.

This cycle is repeated over and over to ensure Bill's productivity level remains as close to his apex as possible.

He is worked, over-worked, and then given an inconsequential reward (like extra vacation days that he really makes up for by working harder on his return). Then, he is worked and over-worked again.

It is much easier for a man like Bill to accept—to be submissive to his environment—than to be the catalyst of change in his environment.

Because Bill is the perfect substitute slave.

And most Bills are white.

Some people will actually subject themselves to all of that for an average wage. But believe it or not, Bill is still more valuable because his productivity and competence will always be at a higher level than someone like that.

Financially free people (black, white, and brown) have paid slaves that are black, white, and brown. Those paid slaves have cheap labor slaves in the third world.

If you live in a developed nation, no matter your color, you have slaves in the third world making your goods.

Does that make Black and Brown Americans racist toward the Chinese who sew their clothes for a dollar a day? No—it simply means they just don't care. Or, at least not enough to make a change to their "Station."

8. Whiteguy believes that, in order to be free, you must have someone in your place doing the labor that the economy requires of you.

I was introduced to paid slavery for the first time during my first official business meeting. I was 23. A friend and I had just started a business, and we were having lunch with a prospective client. About ten minutes into the conversation, the subject of employees came up. We didn't have any employees, but apparently the client did because he said something about a recent hire that stuck in my brain like crazy glue:

"I know you want your employees in debt, but she financed a car at $700.00 per month. That just might be a little too much debt."

You want your employees in debt?

That line replayed in my mind like a scratched record. It opened doors in my mind that exposed hallways I had never been down before.

I heard nothing else this perceived jerk said for the rest of the meeting. I knew I would never do business with a guy like this.

A guy that wants to enslave, not uplift.

A guy who would openly admit that sleaze to two guys he had never met; an idiot.

I didn't know much of anything at that age, but I thought working with a person like that would be bad for my business.

Of course, we did business with him anyway. Partly because my partner didn't see the harm in it, and we needed the money.

After the client slow-paid, then no-paid, and tried to take advantage of us in general, we cut him loose. But I never regretted doing business with him. What I learned in those few months was far more valuable than his money. That experience, especially the "employee in debt" comment, turned a light on in my mind that has influenced every decision I have made since.

Okay, I went on way too long about that. Let's talk about something a little more fun and maybe even controversial. I don't really know, because I'm white.

CHAPTER IV

9. White people love to talk black.

I know what you're thinking: "Duh...and they sound so stupid and naive." Right?

But I'm not talking about the accent that morons use who don't know how bad and offensive it sounds, or when the naive try to act like they're hip or "with it". I'm talking about the accent non-moronic whites use when they are around their closest friends. The one that's so good you might not even believe it. The one that can mimic a specific region.

The one that's a competition.

Some white people turn black when they get mad or excited. They can't even help it.

It seems to roll off the tongue smoothly and expresses a feeling that only *it* could. Whites believe that it conveys a point which could not otherwise be achieved.

Mostly, it's when something important needs to be said with few words. Like, if the smallest guy in the group takes shotgun. You need to quickly convey that: he shouldn't have taken shotgun, the reasons he shouldn't have, that he should have known better, and that he needs to get in the back ASAP.

That would be a lot of white-talk.

"Gitch yo ass in da back, skinny dumbass m-fu**er."

Much more efficient…and fun.

In the white world, talking black conveys a sense of playfulness. Anytime whites want to say something someone else might take offense to, they can just say it in "black", and it's understood to be lighthearted.

Believe it or not, some white friend groups talk "black" half of the time.

This doesn't just go for adults. It applies to all ages

It's very common to have a car load of white kids and adults instantly become black when a choice song comes on or if someone challenges the group with their perfectly cadenced Ebonics response to the drive-thru worker who forgot their fries, regardless of whether the worker was white or black.

Most whites are in silent agreement that it's not to mock or ridicule. It's to have fun and almost celebrate.

You might say that it's still offensive to black people, and it's just plain racist. But, like I said before, we just don't care that much. Would you sacrifice a good time for political correctness? I didn't think so.

White People Think Black People…

Think whites are devious and manipulative by nature.

Think whites miss the fundamental, spiritual point of a lot of issues.

Think whites cannot feel certain visceral emotions that blacks can.

Think their people have been oppressed for so long that they need the help of other cultures for a given period of time before they can be self-governing.

Think they are closer to God than whites.

Have a hatred for whites that is deeper than they can admit or even see.

What White People Do Not Understand About Blacks:

White people do not understand why blacks sometimes paint their front door purple or blue shortly after moving in. Or change the color of the trim/shutters to a more "lively" color. Some whites believe this is some sort of sign, but they do not know for sure.

White people do not understand why some blacks put crowns in the rear windshield of their car.

White people do not understand Ebonics half of the time, but they act like they do.

Whiteguy can't tell if blacks can actually hear and understand each other when they get loud in groups.

10. White People Lie.

If you haven't guessed by now, everything you have read to this point has been a lie. It is simply an example of one strategy used in propaganda.

It is said the best lie is 90 percent truth—to give the feeling of truth—seeming to shoot from the hip—to be blunt and harsh—to project honesty.

The prior pages were designed, first, to give the impression of honesty. Secondly, they were written to sway your opinion of white people.

For example:

The prior section (White people love to talk black) was about seven paragraphs long. All seven paragraphs were true except for two sentences:

"Most whites are in silent agreement that it's not to mock or ridicule. It's to have fun and almost celebrate."

That was the lie.

Saved for almost the end of the section, after the six paragraphs of setup specifically written to make you believe just those two lines.

Of course, it's to ridicule and make fun of.

The "White Station" portion was just a setup to attempt to convince you of how something inherently racist might not be racist. So, at the least, you might even consider the notion. Just a little doubt is enough.

But of course, white people are racist. They have to be. They've been told since birth that they are superior. They are taught a history of white domination and innovation. They see how whites live around the globe, compared to people of color.

How could there be any question?

Whites are racist.

Whites believe that they do not need people of color, but people of color need them.

Whites believe their lives and the lives of their children would be greatly improved in the absence of people of color.

Whites believe most people of color "ruin everything".

Whites believe that Caucasians are the superior race, then Asians, Indians, Middle Easterners, North Africans, and Sub-Saharan Africans… in that order.

Whites do not respect blacks.

As white children grow into young adults, they begin to hear things like "white privilege," "colonization," and "white greed." They begin to discover that other races contributed great innovations to world:

The Chinese invented gun powder.
An African-American invented the multiplex telegraph.
The Egyptians invented the sail.
The list goes on.

They begin to feel a target being stapled to their back.
But that only reinforces their racist tendencies.

Just like in sports, everyone is gunning for number one.

Whites think:

Wow, the Chinese invented gunpowder. "How interesting and clever".

Then they think about the result.

They think about the sail, the telegraph, and everything else. And, again, the result. They feel that the endgame is that the only game, and there is only one winner. It does not matter how you win. It only matters *that* you win. And it especially doesn't matter if you didn't know you were playing a game.

Because you should have.

THE END (not)

So…Was that what you have been thinking since page one? That everything prior to "**10. White people lie**" was a lie? And that what I have said in Section 10 is the truth?

Well, you're wrong. That was a lie too. Please refer to the 90% rule mentioned earlier.

BS?

Nope.

The purpose of this essay is to illustrate a core problem:

ster·e·o·type
ˈsterēəˌtīp/

noun
noun: **stereotype**; plural noun: **stereotypes**
1.
a widely held but fixed and oversimplified image or idea of a particular type of person or thing.

If you felt, at any time during this read, that something rang true, hopefully, you also understand that there is where a problem lies—inside us all.

Of course, not *all* whites think any certain way or can be grouped into 7 shades, just as not all blacks are one way or another. Of course, some whites share various viewpoints with this essay, as do people of many races.

Of course, we are all individuals with a spectrum of opinions, ideals, and insights.

But it's human nature to group people together—to stereotype—to rank and label, then shelve and move on, making easier navigation of oneself and the world—to create an enemy—something to fight against...to blame.

THE END